The Life & Business Philosophy of Austin T. Levy

Visionary Entrepreneur

Edited by
Kenneth Proudfoot

Photographs by
Melanie Madden

Shoreline Press ◆ Rhode Island

Published in the United States by
Shoreline Press (RI)
P.O. Box 110
Slocum, RI 02877

Manufactured in the United States of America

First Edition

ISBN: 1887671056
ISBN-13: 978-1887671057

Dedicated
to my personal heroes
- my parents -
Noel & Henrietta Proudfoot,
who have always inspired
and always believed.

ACKNOWLEDGMENTS

First and foremost I must thank the two women who first believed in this project, Linda Rivet, Research Librarian at the Jesse M. Smith Memorial Library in Harrisville, RI, and Pat Mehrtens, Burrillville Town Historian and author. Without their early encouragement and support, this combination book and documentary film project would not have started or been realized.

Many others encouraged me and supported this effort to capture the history of Austin T. Levy and his best friend, confidant and wife, June Rockwell Levy. These include Betty & Carlo Mencucci at the Burrillville Historical & Preservation Society, historian and writer, Jim Ignasher, Photographer Melanie Madden, Cortland Place Co-Owners Norman Audio, Sr. and Norman Audio, Jr., Cindy Williams at Overlook Nursing & Rehabilitation Center, Tom Kravitz, Burrillville Town Planner, and Christine Langlois, Deputy Planner, Town of Burrillville. Thanks to Alicia Condon, Linda Rivet and Patricia Mehrtens for reviewing drafts of this book. Many thanks to Catherine Sengel for her suggestions and copy editing of the final draft.

Special thanks to Jerry Leveille who has encouraged & supported this work at every step.

I am very grateful for research and development financial support of this project from the Rhode Island Council for the Humanities, the Rhode Island Historical Society, The Bahamas Historical Society, and the June Rockwell Levy Foundation.

As always, I am indebted to my wife and best friend, Ann Marie Marshall, who has from the beginning encouraged and supported the vision for this project and has traveled with me on research trips in Connecticut, throughout Rhode Island, and the Bahamas to research & prepare materials for this book and the accompanying documentary film, *The Amazing Life & Times of Austin T. Levy.*

Austin T. Levy
(1880-1951)

Austin T. Levy was a beloved husband, friend, visionary, musician, entrepreneur, & philanthropist. His God-given gifts for business, critical thinking, and caring for others were well

applied throughout his lifetime, particularly before, during, and after World War I, the Great Depression and World War II.

For every activity he took on, he studied the root of the problems that prevented the most efficient use of the available resources. He then developed workable and, ultimately, profitable and humane solutions.

Preface

Austin T. Levy had three careers. He was a successful textile industrialist, a visionary Bahamas' agriculturist, and a generous philanthropist. But he was much more. Too much to fully tell here. But with everything he accomplished, the world he inhabited became a little richer, a little nicer, and a whole lot happier. I have enjoyed getting to know this man who, though unknown to me two years ago, has become a teacher, mentor, and an inspiration.

Austin T. Levy came into my life through his wife, June Rockwell Levy. Mr. Levy, a successful 20th century textile manufacturer, had named a charitable foundation after his wife. One day I asked where the money for the foundation came from. No one in my circle could tell me. I looked up the foundation name and found a photo of her husband and the source of the foundation's assets. I went to our library web site searching for "Austin T. Levy." A book with that title popped up. It was written by Louis Bleiweis and published in 1953. Mr. Bleiweis was a reporter for *The Woonsocket Call*, a daily newspaper, and spent much time with Mr. Levy. June Rockwell Levy asked him to write her husband's biography following his untimely death in 1951 at the age of 70. In the pages of Mr. Bleiweis's book, I realized that the vision, scope, and accomplishments of Austin T. Levy were both unique and lasting.

My immediate thought was to shoot some video of the people and places that could help showcase and document the life and times of Austin T. Levy. I quickly realized the subject required a more professional treatment as a documentary film that could be broadcast on television and shared through DVDs and classroom programs. With Emmy-winning videographer Jim Karpeichik, a film of Levy's life is in production.

With further reading and research, I found that Levy's ideas and philosophies about business, life, money, wages, profit sharing, government and many other subjects are the keys to understanding his optimistic outlook on life, his great love of people, and his great success in manufacturing, civic improvements, agriculture and philanthropy.

In these pages are gathered the thoughts behind Austin T. Levy's busy life of doing well by doing good. These are the thoughts, beliefs and philosophies of this inspiring leader of the early 20th century.

I hope some of Austin T. Levy's words will inspire you as they have me.

Kenneth Proudfoot
Wickford, Rhode Island
March 2015

Introducing

the Life of

Austin T. Levy

Austin T. Levy (1950)

KENNETH PROUDFOOT

The Mill Dam (1857) and Falls at Harrisville Pond. (MM Photo: 2014)

Introducing Austin T. Levy

- In 1909, Austin T. Levy, a 29-year-old woolen commission agent from New York City, leased a small textile mill in Greenville, Rhode Island from the Waterhouse family. The mill had just 40 looms, but included dyeing and finishing facilities for the cloth the looms produced. This lease marked the founding of Levy's Stillwater Worsted Mills and the beginning of an amazing transformation of how people worked, lived and prospered in the rural Town of Burrillville in northwest Rhode Island.

- Over the next three decades, Levy would buy, build and operate a total of 11 mills in three states, employing more than 2,000 people. He pioneered paid two-week vacations, profit-sharing plans, and a generous employee stock ownership program. Most importantly, Levy recognized the inseparable relationship between the textile mills, workers and their families, and the survival and prosperity of the communities where his mills were sited.

Former home of June Rockwell & Austin T. Levy in Harrisville, RI. (MM Photo: 2014)

- He realized that wage rates, even more than production and profits, were directly tied to the survival and prosperity of the local economy. With this thought always in the back of his mind, Levy kept his mills operating throughout the Great Depression of the 1930s, one of the very few operators to do so. At other times, when textile production increased due to improved technology and labor hours were necessarily reduced, Levy raised the hourly wage so his workers would continue to earn the same amount of weekly pay.

- Levy recognized that his people were the key to the company's profitable growth. He loved the people in his community and was always looking for opportunities to support and encourage his workers and their families to have better lives. He constantly praised his management team, line workers, and everyone else who helped make the company go. And he was happy to share his success with the people he worked with, ultimately selling the business to his employees, many who were already stockholders.

Burrillville Town Building (1933), a gift of the Levy's. (MM Photo: 2014)

- Austin T. Levy also had many other interests apart from the management of Stillwater Worsted Mills. He was an athlete and an avid tennis player, playing well into his 60's. He was an accomplished musician who excelled at the violin and viola. He loved music history and owned a 1709 Stradivarius violin. On Sunday evenings, his home became the setting where he played viola with a string quartet that included his wife, June Rockwell Levy, on violin. He further championed the creation of the Harrisville Glee Club and a dramatic society called The Village Players. Both groups practiced and performed at the Assembly Theatre in Harrisville, RI.

- Introduced to the Bahamas through his wife's family who owned a home in Nassau, Austin T. Levy encountered another project to challenge his business acumen. He found many of the island nation's people, still subjects of the British Empire, with little or no access to fresh food, including vegetables, milk, eggs, and poultry. After considerable study of the Bahamas soil, weather, and the availability of farm equipment and other tools, he arranged the purchase of 2,000 acres on the island of Eleuthera.

The former No. 4 Mill (1911) on the Clear River in Harrisville, RI. (MM Photo: 2014)

- There Levy bought and shipped earth-moving and farm equipment to the island, transported a herd of dairy cows from the Sherman Farm in Harrisville, built chicken coops, and hired local people to plant, harvest, and process fresh food. Levy later ordered special boats built to ship his fresh milk, eggs, chickens, and ice cream to Nassau. These boats made two trips daily to the capital city on New Providence Island, arriving at Levy's Harrisville Company pier and warehouse in Nassau Harbor. He built 10 Milk Stands around the city where residents could purchase his fresh products on a daily basis.

- Less known was Austin T. Levy's interest and participation in Republican politics in Rhode Island. While a lifelong Republican, he did not get involved in Rhode Island Republican Party activities until 1934. He was elected chairman of the Burrillville Republican Town Committee in 1936 and in 1938 managed the successful statewide campaign of William H. Vanderbilt for Rhode Island Governor (1939-41).

Harrisville Gazebo and First Universalist Church (1886). (MM Photo: 2014)

- Though he was well known in the northwestern part of the state, Levy was not as recognized in the rest of Rhode Island, particularly in the urban areas of Pawtucket, Providence, and Cranston. Nevertheless, he began asking for advice and feedback from his friends and business colleagues on whether he should run for the U.S. Senate. His opponent would be the then current governor, Democrat John O. Pastore. In the 1950 election, Levy won the vote in 21 of Rhode Island's 39 cities and towns, but Pastore won in the largest cities and was elected Senator.

- The Levy's retreated to Nassau to rest and recuperate following the exhausting campaign. They soon returned to Rhode Island via New York where he had a health check-up and then six weeks in a New York hospital. During the last week of October, Levy's health declined and he entered Jane Brown Hospital in Rhode Island. Austin T. Levy passed away on a rainy autumn day in Providence on November 24, 1951. He was 70 years old.

Another view of the Mill Dam (1857) and Falls at Harrisville Pond. (MM Photo: 2014)

- In the Town of Burrillville, Austin T. and June Rockwell Levy left an enduring impact on the villages of Harrisville and Pascoag. The construction and gift of the Burrillville Town Buildng, Ninth District Court of Rhode Island, the Assembly Theatre, the Jesse M. Smith Memorial Library (now the Town Hall Annex), U.S. Post Offices in Harrisville and Pascoag, a modern indoor ice skating rink and the former Burrillville High School were among projects they spearheaded, funded and supported.

- All of these buildings – several now converted to meet changing community needs – are still open and being used by the residents of Burrillville and its surrounding communities.

June Rockwell Levy
June 14, 1886 – August 8, 1971
The best friend and wife of Austin T. Levy

Beliefs and Ideals

Austin T. Levy

If Mr. Levy had not done anything else
in his business career except share his beliefs and ideals
about life and work and teach the meanings of them to
the people around him, he would have been considered a
successful man.

What helped make him extremely successful
was taking the heartfelt content of his talks and speeches
and applying it to everybody and everything in his life:
family, friends, business, community, state and nation.

Austin T. Levy expounded on the intertwined theme
of beliefs and idealism at the Sixth Semi-Annual Profit
Sharing Meeting with his employees on
July 17, 1918 in Harrisville, RI.

Every Worker's Business

It is perhaps not sufficiently understood,
that a man working for wages conducts a business, much in the
same way that a man does who maintains a shop, or lawyer
who maintains an office.

Austin T. Levy, speaking to the
Boston Council of Social Agencies, Boston. (1933)

What Makes The Difference Between Men?

Why is one man different from another?

It isn't because he is taller or stronger.
It isn't even because he is smarter.

The main difference in men is the difference
in the things they believe in; the things they stand for.

Idealism in Business

Let me outline what an ideal business condition might be.
I think you will agree that it would be an equally ideal condition
for workers in any other field. By workers I mean all those
engaged in enterprise, whether they are employed by others or
employ others, or pursue their enterprises individually.

1. Working conditions kept always in step with the newest
    development.
2. Hours of labor tuned to the greatest efficient
    productiveness of the individual.
3. Adequate wage for efficient productiveness.
4. The greatest possible elimination of waste, whether of
    effort or materials.
5. The proper sort of personal contact.
6. Co-operative ownership in the results of the effort.

*Austin T. Levy, at the National Federation for Child Study in
New York City. (November, 1913)*

Practicality & Idealism

It will be conceded that the essences of an idealism are an impersonal reverence for the thing to be accomplished, and the subordination of self on the part of those who seek to further it.

There is nothing about idealism that takes it out of harmony with practical accomplishment.

Indeed no great practical movement in the development of the race has ever succeeded or been established without the impetus of a high idealism behind it, and likewise no great leap forward step in human progress has ever been made excepting by men who placed the object of their efforts far beyond any personal considerations of their own.

Importance of Ideals & Beliefs

A man without ideals and without beliefs that he is ready to fight for, to stand up for, that man doesn't amount to much. That is the man who never accomplishes much. He does that because he doesn't believe in anything.

Now, most people do and no progress has ever been made in the world, no great movement has ever been undertaken in the whole world except it was founded and based on the beliefs of some man's or group of men's ideals.

Ideals & Beliefs in Action

Take the case of Jesus, for instance, whose belief
and ideal was the establishment of the brotherhood of man.

He had no great physical power;
He had no great army,
but He had the force of that ideal and that ideal
was powerful to the extent that He believed and
He made it powerful to the extent that He believed in it,
and ever since His time the world has been struggling to
bring into execution his ideal of the brotherhood of man.

Idealism Expressed in Work

You know that in every locality there are men who
have the reputation of doing a good job, whether it is building a
home, fixing a road, or whatever their work in life might be.

You will find numerous individuals who have the name among
people who know them of doing a good job, and then you
know other men in the same neighborhood who have the
reputation of never doing anything right.

The man who is doing good work is expressing his idealism.
He is putting a certain amount of his ---- into that work.
The other man doesn't care.
He has no idealism.

Idealism: A Powerful Force for Profit

Now, it is a curious thing that while idealism is being
scoffed at, it is about the most powerful force for
profit that can enter into any business.

If the business is idealized by all the people who take part
in it, their product must of necessity approach an ideal
product. There must be less mistakes, less mishaps.

It is a better article,
whatever the article may be,
than a similar article.

Idealism in Creating a Better Community

What would be an ideal community?

An ideal community would be one where the work turned out in it would be the best work made anywhere; where the people in that community had more fun than they had in any other community; where they had more interest in their lives; where they had the best homes and the best general community lives.

The Role of the Idealist

The ideals of men and groups of men have been
[important] in the development of the world.

Now an idealist for a long time has been a man that has been
laughed at. He has been scorned. He was a dreamer.
There was nothing practical about him, but yet these [people]
have established things that were intensely practical.

They put their finger on the mainsprings of human life and
affected their cause, and while no great human event can take
place without the background of idealism, no real idealist – I do
not mean a faddist – no real idealist ever leaves
the world without having left something of value behind him.

Idealism is an Individual Expression

It doesn't make any difference how apparently humble a man's task in life may be. If it is only to dig a ditch, to lay a pipe, he can do that with a certain expression of himself that makes the difference between himself and the man who has no ideals.

He can dig the ditch poorly; he can dig it well.
A man can keep records poorly or he can keep them well.
A man can finish cloth poorly or he can finish it well.

There is no occupation in life in which this vital force of idealism is not the controlling factor.

The main reason and the only valid reason for making good cloth is that the man's idealism must be expressed in making good work and he will not allow himself to make bad work. If he is an honest man he must automatically satisfy everybody else who looks at his work.

Work • Life • Money

Austin T. Levy

Austin T. Levy believed in setting the right priorities for one's life, family, business and community. As prosperous as he became during his 40+ year career, he knew what really mattered and he shared his thoughts, beginning with his employees and managers, and continuing with his neighbors, business colleagues, politicians, and world leaders.

Built originally as the Jesse M. Smith Memorial Library (1933), this building now serves as the Burrillville Town Hall Annex. (Photo: 2014)

The Purpose of Enterprise

The purpose of all enterprise is to
supply human wants and one of the
first functions of any enterprise is to
contribute something to the well-being
of the people who carry it on, and
to the community of which it is a part.

The Wage Earner's Main Objective

It is doubtful that many business enterprises
clearly define their own objectives, but the wage
earner's objective is quite definite in his own mind.

If I understand that objective,
it is day to day satisfaction of living,
with some provision for future security.

It is a legitimate objective.

March 24, 1937

Unskilled Labor

…there isn't any such thing
as unskilled labor.

Now if you think so,
I will defy anyone to go out
and dig a ditch and dig it well.
I know. I have tried it.

Levy, in an address to the Plantations Club,
Providence, RI (1921)

Working

Then you hear about people
working for you.

Well, if they work for you,
they work with their hands and feet;
if they work *with* you,
they work with their heads and hearts;
and there is quite a difference.

Austin T. Levy, in an address to the
Plantations Club
Providence, R.I. (1921)

Making Money is Not Enough

No business that makes money
and merely makes money is a success.

If that is all we make we are a failure,
and I say the things we should make here
are an ideal product
and an ideal community.

July 17, 1918

Work & Life

Work is not an incident to life.
Life is an incident to work.

Life is the biggest thing, not work,
but you cannot live without work.

August 19, 1920

Worst Two Words

There are two words
in our whole vocabulary
that I hate
worse than all the others.

One of them is Charity
and other one is Poverty,
and you do not have charity
unless you have poverty,
and that is why I hate charity.

August 19, 1920

Different Goals

Bolshevism feeds and thrives on poverty,
on hunger and on misery.

Now our program is just the opposite.
Instead of everybody being poor
we want to see if everyone cannot be rich.

August 19, 1920

Ethical Profit

We can agree, I think, that people engage in business for profit,
and that it cannot be carried on without; but it is a fact,
not generally understood and perhaps beyond the spiritual
grasp of the majority – but nevertheless a fact – that
that conduct of business which answers the
highest ethical conception is productive
of the greatest material gain.

September 17, 1932

Philosophy of Business

The obligations of business are quite plain.
Whether they wish it or not, those who control business are
responsible for its conduct and for its influence on the present
and future of society…Out of the wealth of its experience, it
might have stated its aim, its powers and opportunities, its
restrictions and limitations, its influence, its obligations
and responsibilities.

We may consider…what such a
Philosophy of Business might embrace.

*Austin T. Levy, speaking to the Eastern Convention of the
Unitarian Laymen's League, 1932*

Philosophy of Business

•To provide ways of life that are interesting,
satisfying and secure for those who take part in it.

•To make available things and services
that people find useful.

•To create a profit of sufficient size to carry
out these two aims and to provide for its perpetuation
in such amended forms as its future may require.

*Austin T. Levy, speaking to the Eastern Convention of the
Unitarian Laymen's League. (1932)*

The Great Depression

It is said that we are passing through hard times.
Nonsense.
These are good times because they are providing the obstacles
which our youth will conquer and through which they will
make themselves dependable men and women. They are good
times because through them we will come again to a proper
sense of things that are worthwhile; -- and, if because of this
period we shall achieve a re-birth of those spiritual impulses
that made this nation great, then these will be the best times
that this people has ever seen.

Our national distress may then be our
national opportunity…

Austin T. Levy, speaking to the Eastern Convention of the
Unitarian Laymen's League, 1932

Economic Recovery in a Depression

There can be no recovery until
general employment is reestablished in our land.

Other national problems cannot be disposed of
until this one is set straight and when that is accomplished,
all of the others will be on their way to
fall in line of themselves.

Broadly speaking, we have no other problems.

*Austin T. Levy, speaking to the U.S. Senate Committee on
the Judiciary (February 1935)*

The Bane of Unemployment

Government spending and unemployment compensation
will not correct unemployment. They will merely put off and
aggravate the day of reckoning.

I propose that a running inventory or census of National
unemployment can be made the basis for providing a prompt
and effective means for bringing the main factors of our economic
life into a comfortable working relationship with one another,
and for keeping them there.

We must always have a certain amount of floating unemployment in
our country to provide the reserves of man hours that are needed.
But there is a vast difference between necessary reserves and
crushing surpluses, and we know from bitter experiences that when
we have 10 or 12 million unemployed we are
in serious trouble.

Austin T. Levy, 1933

The Key to the National Dilemma

It seems to me that all of the questions of the day are corridors in the labyrinth of our National dilemma and that the key is an open sesame for them all.

It is the key that the world mislays from time to time, groping along its painful and uncertain way until it can again be found. It is the key on which all philosophies are based and around which all associations of men and women cling. It is nothing other than the maintenance of proper human relations, based on fair dealing, good will, courtesy and consideration. Men and governments may come and go, but the need for these is eternal.

Speaking before the members of
St. Michael's Brotherhood and guests.
January 22, 1934
Excerpt from *The Parish Monthly*, January 1934

Business Goals Beyond Profit

1- The material and well-being of the
people connected with it.

2- The conservation and advancement
of the common interest.

3- The present and future of the state.

Speech at the Faculty Club
Brown University
Providence, RI

April 29, 1936

Wages

Austin T. Levy (1950)

Austin T. Levy was adamant throughout his life that the economy could be improved by raising wage rates. He made many speeches, printed pamphlets, testified before the U.S. Congress, and even placed full-page advertisements in the textile industry's daily trade newspaper calling on his industry colleagues to both reduce the number of hours in the work week and raise wage rates.

Here follow some of his many
philosophies and beliefs
on this subject.

Wages & Hours

I am in favor of maximum hours, not left to anybody's discretion, but to be determined by the facts of employment in the United States.

As to a minimum wage, you can put one on, and make it as high as you please – I don't care; but if you keep the unemployment where it belongs, the people themselves will see to it that they are properly paid.

You can only beat down people when there is large unemployment. I do not object to a minimum wage if anybody wants it – only make it high enough. But get the employment going and have it so steady that people may confidently count on it from year to year.

Speaking on the Proposed Wages & Hour Bill
Joint Labor Committee, Washington, DC
June 10, 1937

Low Wages & High Wages

What are high wages and what are low wages?

Wages are high when they enable the wage earner
to conduct his business successfully and they are low when
they do not permit him to do this.

Stated another way, wages are high when they
provide enough money to purchase what is efficiently
produced, and wages are low when they are insufficient
to purchase production.

Living Wages

For a long time a yardstick for fixing wages was called, variously, 'subsistence wages,' 'living wages,' or 'minimum wages.' It was thought that working people should be paid only so much as they must have to live, on some low and debatable scale. Low wages were regarded as a matter of concern for those who received them, without much idea that they might be detrimental to the interests of those who paid them.

It seems clear that we are no longer interested in any low form of wages by whatever name, and we should think instead in terms of Standards of Living as they evolve from time to time; --- with the belief that working people must share in these standards as the only means for sustaining them; --- and with the discernment by those who pay wages, that unless these standards are advanced from time to time to absorb our increasing production their enterprises will perish.

Living Wages

The desired living standards for any year will prevail, when the people of the United States are able to purchase, afford, and enjoy all that these same people can produce in a work week of a given length, with every technical aid they are able to command.

An ever higher standard of living for all its people is the only means by which the world's constantly expanding production can be absorbed. It is the only preventative for large scale unemployment. It is the surest path to peace.

Austin T. Levy, 1950

Embracing Higher Wages

It seems self-evident that a civilization that demands and intends to supply a fairly abundant life must be based on a scale of wages that is higher than any scale that prevailed when life was less abundant.

The common objection to high wages is the belief on the part of those who pay them that they cannot afford to pay more than they do, and that the things that are made cannot be sold if wages are advanced.

Embracing Higher Wages

In the first place, high wages do not necessarily mean high costs. This is not well understood. Secondly, there is nothing sacrosanct about a wage scale, or wholesale or retail prices; and those who say that high wages prevent their doing business, must have short memories.

And everyone knows that people who choke over a 10 per cent wage increase, swallow a 30 per cent rise in the cost of raw materials without a murmur; and in many industries a 30 percent raise in the cost of materials is equal to a 50 percent wage increase or not.

Wage Rates & the Unemployed

A wage rate means nothing at all to a man who is out of work and it means very little more to a man who has unemployment for only one or two days a week.

There is no person…who could order his existence and budget the life of his family on a minimum hourly rate for his services with the number of hours unknown.

(1935)

Profitable Wages

By profitable wages
I mean wages that are greater
than the cost of securing them.

(1933)

Payments to the Unemployed

Payments of money to the unemployed and their dependents may be immediately necessary to avoid actual want, but they do not answer the question.

The American people do not want relief.

They want occupation, and the spiritual and economic independence that can come only through occupation and reasonable assurance of its continuance.

Speaking before the Senate Committee
on the Judiciary
Washington, D.C.

February 6, 1935

Profitable Wages

Remember that while wages have increased during the
past 25 years, the average output per worker has
increased more than wages.

Therefore, the contribution to society of the
individual worker is greater per dollar of wages
than it has ever been before.

(1936)

WAGES

◆

The next change in wages will be upward.

◆

A constructive step -- the whole nation will benefit.

◆

*Prudent manufacturers will provide for
this in the prices of their goods.*

◆

*Our Company will welcome the change
and will take part in it when it comes.*

◆

STILLWATER WORSTED MILLS

Advertising copy Mr. Levy placed in the Daily Record, a New York City
textile trade newspaper, to promote his call for higher wages

20 DAILY NEWS RECORD, WEDNESDAY, JUNE 12, 1935

The greatest assistance that industry can now render to itself and to the nation is a prompt and substantial wage increase.

No other thing can so immediately and conclusively establish that American business is ready and able to provide the leadership for which the situation calls, and that it has confident faith in its own and the country's future.

STILLWATER WORSTED MILLS

Facsimile of an advertisement placed by Mr. Levy in the Daily Record,
a textile trade newspaper, to promote higher wages

Incentives & Benefits

Austin T. Levy

Austin T. Levy was a visionary who implemented
plans and programs he saw as necessary for the betterment
of his employees and his business and his community.

Most impressive was his creation and implementation
of profit sharing, two-week paid vacations,
and employee stock ownership.

To American Business

Our Nation is committed to, and determined
to have a 1936 kind of civilization.

Our Nation has the resources to supply and maintain such a
civilization, and business as now constituted cannot endure
unless their resources are utilized.

Such a civilization resulting from the free utilization of the
National resources can be maintained only if the incomes
of people are sufficient to support it.

It is up to business to establish wage scales that will
support the civilization to which the Nation is now committed.

Daily News Record, Monday, November 9, 1936, page 5*

◆

**This was one of many full-page advertisements Austin T. Levy placed in the New York
trade press to rally the business community, specifically the textile industry, to
raise wages to improve the consumer economy during the Great Depression.*

Profit-Sharing

For many, many years, it has been thought that when one man employed many others, that those who employed and those who were employed had nothing in common. And so it became almost a custom for employers to pay just as little as they had to, and for work people to give their labor only as much as they were made to.

Now our company has felt somewhat differently about this thing. We believe that there is everything in common between our work and ourselves.

We believe that if the company has prosperity that the work people should share in that prosperity, and we also believe that if every man and woman connected with the company has something to gain by increasing the profits, that each one will do his utmost to make the profits as large as possible.

Austin T. Levy, speaking to the Stillwater family about
implementing a profit-sharing plan. (1916)

Profit Sharing Explained

We have just two reasons in our company for sharing profits.
Firstly, because we think it is a fair thing to do;
we think that everybody who helps to create
a profit should share in it.

The other reason is that we expect to make
money by profit sharing.

We believe that where everybody has an incentive to
make the profits as large as possible that they
will do their best to accomplish that.

July 17, 1918

Does Profit Sharing Work?

Other men in business have asked me
whether profit sharing pays.

They know that our company has distributed in the
aggregate a very large sum of money as profit share –
and my answer has been this – that all through the
war [WWI], at no time did a machine in our mill stand
idle for the need of a man to run it. Whether that
was because of profit-sharing or for some other
cause I cannot tell, but we think it is.

Community Consciousness

Levy's company was based in Harrisville, RI and he needed more production capacity. Levy was aware that many times a business enlarged or located its operation in a community without taking into account the possible consequences of that action.

Almost always such industrial developments are attended by profound changes in the social and cultural aspects of the locality in which they take place. Sometimes these changes have been advantageous to the community.

Oftentimes they have not.

After a detailed study, Levy concluded that business expansion in Harrisville was to be avoided as there was insufficient housing, schools, and services to support such expansion. It would also alter the rural nature of the community.

He proposed his idea of establishing a mill in another community that might benefit and profit from having the business located there. After presenting the plan to the company's management staff, it was agreed to purchase the Bethel Mill in Ashaway, Rhode Island. (1925)

Housing for Mill Workers

In 1918, Levy wanted to build and rent homes to the workers in the mills.
He realized, even before beginning the project that the prevailing wages of
a working man were insufficient to support the rental cost of a new home.

It was clear that there would have to be a new approach to this matter, or consideration of a housing project would have to be abandoned. The decision was made on the following reasoning:

When a loom or any other machine is placed on a mill floor, the first consideration is not that it must return a certain rental for the space that it occupies, but it must be installed for its best operating efficiency.

Housing for Mill Workers

If this is true of the machine, is it not even more important
with respect to the man who operates the machine?

Without the man the machine would be useless.

*On this line of reasoning the house construction went forward and
rentals were based not on cost, but on what the prospective tenant's earnings enabled
him to pay. This meant that there could be no direct profits from this housing.
But through the years Levy believed the indirect returns more than justified the
venture. The company built 22 seven-room houses in North Hill in the village
of Harrisville. Within six months, the housing development included trees,
a sewage system, and roads.*

Decentralization of Industry

Of course industry exerts a profound influence on the society of which it is a part. That is something from which there is no escape.

It has been a common practice for industry to locate or enlarge in a locality that seemed advantageous, without a clear understanding of the consequences.

Almost always such industrial developments are attended by profound changes in the social and cultural aspects of the locality in which they take place. Sometimes these changes have been advantageous. Oftentimes they have not.

◆

These thoughts guided Levy as his business grew.
In the early 1920's, Levy needed to expand his production capacity. Realizing that expansion in Harrisville would change the rural character of the village and put undue pressure on housing, school facilities, and other municipal services, he decided to develop his expansion plans elsewhere.

On Unions

Austin T. Levy

…any man was free to belong to a union if he chose,
and also that any man was free to work without being a
member of a union if he so chose; that the company was glad
and ready at all times to receive anyone, either individually or in
groups, respecting anything concerning the operation of the
mill, but that the company would not countenance coercion in
the cause of union membership, or in any other cause;
in other words, the rights and beliefs of every individual
must be respected.

March 4, 1921

Education

Austin T. Levy

Austin T. Levy was educated as most boys were
in the latter fifth of the 19th century.
He left school at 16 to begin work
as a $3 per week office clerk.

But he clearly valued education
and the power of knowledge.

The First Function of Education

Now, we used to think that the first business,
the first function of education was to teach children reading, writing
and arithmetic. That is, of course, a very important business, a very
important function for education. But the main value of education in a
broader sense is to enable a man to decide for himself, to think over in
his own mind what are the things in life that he believes in, what are the
things that he individually values -- what are the things that to him are
worthwhile. Every human being has to elect that for himself. That is the
privilege and the value of his education, that should enable him to decide
those points intelligently and with good reason.

July 17, 1918 : Harrisville, RI

Pursuing Higher Standards

I say that if we can achieve a generally
higher standard of education and
standard of living,
we will steadily make more
contributions to the cause of America.

July 23, 1919

Politics & Government

Austin T. Levy

Austin T. Levy was active in politics during the latter third of his life. In 1950, he was convinced by the state Republican party to run for U.S. Senate against Rhode Island Governor John O. Pastore. Levy knew the battle would be hard and not likely to be successful. But in typical fashion he put in a serious effort but was ultimately defeated due mostly to being much less known than the sitting governor. With his friend Louis Bleiweis he outlined his reasons for running. Some of his other thoughts about government are included here.

Running for U.S. Senator – The Why

I have always felt keenly the great debt that each
one of us owes to this fair land of ours and it seemed to
me that with such experiences as I may now possess,
the time had come for me to help in the problems
that lie ahead.

Fall 1950

Running for U.S. Senator – The What

If I am sent to Washington [as Rhode Island's Senator]
I shall carry with me a determined interest in the things for
which I have worked through the years – the well-being of a
self-reliant people, and the fulfillment of our nation's destiny.

It is my conviction that our country's future can only be
assured through the prosperity; happiness and economic
independence of the great mass of the people.

Fall 1950

Thoughts on Government

Remember that the proper aim of the government
is not the control of government,
but the service of people.

(1936)

Government Regulations

Relinquish the philosophy of "You may not."
Adopt instead the spirit of "Let's go!"

(1936)

Government Spending

Stop unnecessary, injudicious, wasteful spending.
You wouldn't do it if it were your own money.

(1936)

Money & Government

Don't imagine that the
American electorate can be bought.

When such a thing is possible,
it won't be worth buying.

(1936)

Land of Opportunity

Wherever power lies,
either in the hand of Government or in private keeping,
there lies also the responsibility for holding open
in this fair land of ours, the channels of individual
opportunity, through which men of every station
can attain to self-reliance.

When these channels are definitely closed
our Country will cease to be.

January 4, 1937

Leadership

Just what do we expect of leadership?

It seems to me that leadership has
three major functions:

1- To recognize what is needed

2- To devise plans for meeting the needs.

3- To see that the plans are operated successfully.

To be competent, leadership
must satisfy all three of these functions.

June 5, 1940

Leadership

Just what does leadership mean?

Leadership may be broadly defined as the relationship between an individual and a group, which revolves about some common interest. If the dominant individual holds his power by custom or law he becomes the agent of authority, and the group consists not of followers, but of subordinates.

A true relation of leadership exists only when a group follows an individual from choice, for its own anticipated advantage.

May 15, 1936

The Future

As you prosper, so must your people.

As a man goes on in life, there comes a time when he begins to slip. He doesn't know it. His friends do not tell him, but if he stays on in a business of which he has been the mainspring he ruins the business.

It is important, therefore, that as they grow older [those] who head such enterprises give some thought and make some provisions against the days when their own activities must lessen and finally cease.

After all, people don't own wealth;
they are merely custodians of it during their lifetimes.

October, 1950

America Matters

Austin T. Levy

Austin T. Levy was a first generation American,
the son of an immigrant father and a first-generation
American mother.
He was parentless before his 16th birthday and raised
by an aunt. But he saw opportunity in America and pursued
the American dream.

With much thought, work, and good decisions,
he pursued a successful future.

He believed in America and his amazing success is a
tribute to his work and his legacy is a reminder that the
American dream is real.

America

My forebears came to this country 110 years ago.

They found what every other family that ever came here
found – opportunities not open to them in Europe.

They played their part in the development of the country.

*Excerpt from a statement by Austin T. Levy, during his 1950 run for the
U.S. Senate as a Republican against Governor John Pastore.*

The Future of America

I want, with you, today to look a little bit
into the future, if we can.

What of the future?

The future of America,
as I see it, is our future,
and the future of America,
as I see it, depends on
America's working people –
people like you and me.

July 23, 1919

Contributing to America's Future

What does America expect of us;
what does she want of us;
what is our greatest value to America?

Now that citizen is of the greatest value to America who contributes most to her institutions – that is, her institutions already established, or those which the future will establish – the man or woman who develops the country in institutions of liberty, free speech, free thought, material helpfulness. Those are American institutions and the man is of most value to his country that develops those institutions and contributes to his country in that way.

July 23, 1919

America's Future

...I shall carry with me a determined interest in the things for which I have worked – the well-being of a self-reliant people and the fulfillment of our nation's destiny.

It is my conviction that our country's future can only be assured through the prosperity, happiness and economic independence of the great mass of the people.

Which Way Now?

There is some body of opinion that as a nation we have been
living too expensively; that we have had too any luxuries
and that we must return to the simpler ways of living that
were current many years ago.

I do not hold with this idea; it is impossible.

The world does not undo its progress.
The world learns to use wisely
whatever it may evolve.

April 6, 1933

American Citizenship

We here in the United States are an amalgamation of
many people -- but whatever our background, our ancestry,
our antecedents, we are all here as the expression of a
common impulse.

Each one of us is here because somewhere in his background
his forebears wanted what we have here, something to be
found nowhere else in all the world.

Freedom of thought; freedom of expression;
freedom of worship; freedom of opportunity.

In one word, Freedom –
that is what our citizenship means.

September 23, 1939

Realities of Ownership

The possession of things that man acquire, whether material or intangible, is called ownership. As such it is but a temporary thing. It continues until the vicissitudes of Life, or Death itself, bring it to an end.

So those who claim ownership in reality only exercise a trusteeship. But so long as it endures, there attaches to all ownership, or trusteeship of this kind, a certain something from which it cannot be separated; i.e., responsibility for its use. And with this responsibility comes responsibility's inseparable partner – Opportunity.

Speaking before the members of
St. Michael's Brotherhood and guests.
January 22, 1934

Excerpted from *The Parish Monthly*, January 1934

Timeline

of the Life of a

Visionary

Austin T. Levy

Austin T. Levy: Timeline of a Social Entrepreneur

Born December 16, 1880
New York City, NY

1884	Theodore Levy, Austin T. Levy's father, passes away
1891	Jahannah Offenheim, Austin T. Levy's mother, passes away
1894-6	Graduates from Grammar School 69 ; Completes one year at City College, NY
1896	Gets first job – Office boy for linen importer: $3/week
1905	First meets June Rockwell in Bristol, RI
1909	Leases Greenville Mill from the Waterhouse family
1909	Founds a new firm named Stillwater Worsted Company
1912	Leases Harrisville Mill from Tinkham family
1913	Gives *Idealism in Business* speech at National Federation for Child Study (NYC)
1913	Moves to Harrisville, RI to better oversee mill
1915	Marries June Rockwell in an Ardmore, PA ceremony
1916	Hires full-time industrial nurse for company
1916	Levy sets forth company's first profit-sharing plan

Austin T. Levy: Socially Conscious Entrepreneur

1918	Builds 22 seven-room houses in North Hill in Harrisville
1920	Builds small home – Ship Ahoy – in Nassau, Bahamas.
1921	Purchases Harrisville Mill from Tinkham family
1921	Speaks to Plantations Club (Providence, RI) about profit sharing plan
1921	180 employees (of 320) strike; Levy closes mill for 30 days
1921	Forms Rhode Island Trio in Harrisville with three world-famous musicians.
1921	Harrisville Glee Club formed, under direction of Alexander Rihm.
1921	The Village Players formed, under direction of Olaf Hauge.
1924	Stock ownership in company is inaugurated
1925	Bethel Mill at Ashaway, RI is acquired
1925	Builds new textile mill at East Woodstock, CT
1925	Purchases Greenville Mill
1926	Acquires two mills in Mapleville, RI
1928	Begins construction of three mills in Virginia, at Augusta Springs, Goshen, and Craigsville, all in the Valley of the Little Calf Pasture.

Austin T. Levy: Socially Conscious Entrepreneur

October, 1929   Stock market crash; Levy mills continue operating

1930's   Employment averages 48 weeks/year. Company makes money every year.

Sept 17, 1932   Makes speech – Aristocracy of Business – to Unitarian Laymen's League

1933   Burrillville Town Buildings project undertaken. Gifts from June and Austin Levy to the Town of Burrillville.

1933   Makes speech – Profitable Wages

1934   Presents his Plan for Control of Unemployment

February, 1935   Makes address – Failure of National Industry Recovery Act – to Senate Commission on Judiciary

1935   Textile mill at Nasonville acquired.

1935   Proposes giving Harrisville land and building for a new high school.

1935   Clear River moved 300 feet to accommodate a larger athletic field for the high school.

1936   Mill at Glendale added to the Stillwater company.

1936   Buys 2,000 acres on Hatchet Bay, Island of Eleuthera, Bahamas

Austin T. Levy: Socially Conscious Entrepreneur

1936	Elected Chairman of the Republican Town Committee, Burrillville; Named President-Elector of Governor Alfred M. Landon
1936	Thirty prefabricated homes built on the Stockwell Farm in Glendale
1937	Vacation with pay is proposed; two weeks' vacation with four weeks' pay. Temporary travel agency set up in the mill office.
1937	Speaks to Congress on Wages and Hours Bill
1937	Frank H. Potter Bridgeway constructed in Pascoag, RI
1937	Proposes Town of Burrillville adopt zoning ordinances to define its business, industrial and residential future. Proposal tabled in 1938, permanently.
1938	Manages Republican State Campaign for William H. Vanderbilt. GOP sweeps state.
1940	Democrats returned to power in Rhode Island
1942	Citing price increases during WWII, Mr. Levy raises wages of all workers on island of Eleuthera, Bahamas and in Nassau

Austin T. Levy: Socially Conscious Entrepreneur

August 24, 1942	Levy sells 11 mills – Harrisville, Mapleville, Glendale, Nasonville, Greenville, Ashaway, Washington, East Woodstock, Augusta Springs, Craigsville, and Goshen – to a new corporation, Harrisvile Combing Company.
1946	Manages Murphy-for-Governor campaign. Murphy loses.
1948	Stillwater Woolen Mills establishes RI scholarship at RISD.
1949	June Rockwell Levy Foundation announced gift of $40,000 to the U.S. Government for the construction of a new post office in Harrisville.
January, 1950	Part 4 of Truman's Speech to Congress mirrors Levy's successful work in the Bahamas
1950	Runs for U.S. Senate seat against Governor Pastore. Though Levy gets a plurality in 21 of the state's 39 cities and towns, he loses by nearly 70,000 votes.
1950	June & Austin travel to Nassau to rest following the election. (Post-November)
August, 1951	Levy enters hospital for checkup; he stays for 6 weeks.
October, 1951	Returns to hospital for second exam.
November 2, 1951	Levy enters Jane Brown Hospital, Providence.

Austin T. Levy: Socially Conscious Entrepreneur

November 24, 1951   Austin t. Levy dies at age 70 at Providence

November 27, 1951   Memorial Service for Austin T. Levy in The Assembly

November 24, 1952   Ground broken for U.S. Post Office in Pascoag, RI

September 1953   Pascoag U.S. Post Office dedicated and presented to U.S. Government by June Rockwell Levy

September 14, 1953   Dedication ceremony of a plaque honoring Austin T. Levy.

August 8, 1971   June Rockwell Levy dies at age 85

The plaque at the grave site of Austin T. Levy reads:

He Loved Life and His Fellow Man
and Gave His Best to Both.

Austin T.

and

June Rockwell Levy's

Amazing Second Act

Austin T. & June Rockwell Levy in the Bahamas

The Levy's had a small winter home in Nassau on the island of New Providence in the Bahamas. It was while visiting there that the humane Levy's noted the lack of available dairy products for the islanders. Levy immediately began experiments to assess the islands' agricultural potential that had previously shown little farm development. This led to the purchase of 2,000 acres of undeveloped land on the island of Eleuthera and the introduction of a dairy herd, Rhode Island Red chickens, and the development of a thriving dairy and poultry operation.

The operation, named The Harrisville Company, was based at Hatchet Bay and included 600 head of cattle, 60,000 hens, and investments in a sales agency, a 10-store chain of milk stands in Nassau, boat lines, a stevedoring firm and a power company.

In 1950, The Harrisville Company was valued at over six million dollars.

For the rest of the story, watch for the coming release of the documentary, *The Amazing Life & Times of Austin T. Levy.* See: www.austintlevyfilm.com for details.

ABOUT THE BOOK

The true author of this volume is Austin T. Levy.

I hope this book will be seen as a respectful homage to the comments, writings, and proclamations he made during his business and personal life. The content in the previous pages was excerpted and edited from the hundreds of thousands of words he wrote and delivered during his very active life, particularly through the writings of *Woonsocket Call* reporter and author of Austin T. Levy (1953), Louis Bleiweis.

What I have found during the past two years learning about Austin T. Levy is how thoughtful, positive, and determined he was to improve the life of those he worked with, lived with, and loved. One book cannot fully capture the full scope of his life, times, and achievements. There are many more stories, events, images, and successes that will be shared in a future book about the amazing life and times of Austin T. Levy.

Meanwhile, watch for the 2015 release of the genesis of this entire project, the writing and filming of a documentary about his life. Go to: www.austintlevyfilm.com.

You can watch the film trailer at https://www.youtube.com/watch?v=00_5CbmpvjM

ABOUT THE EDITOR

Kenneth Proudfoot is a writer, musician, teacher, and filmmaker.

♫

Please send your comments, additions, corrections, and suggestions to:

kennethproudfoot@hotmail.com

Made in the USA
Middletown, DE
08 April 2015